HAL•LEONARD
INSTRUMENTAL
PLAY-ALONG

TEN

MW00812107

Christmas Carols

Arranged by Peter Deneff

HOW TO USE THE CD ACCOMPANIMENT:
A MELODY CUE APPEARS ON THE RIGHT CHANNEL ONLY. IF YOUR
CD PLAYER HAS A BALANCE ADJUSTMENT, YOU CAN ADJUST THE
VOLUME OF THE MELODY BY TURNING DOWN THE RIGHT CHANNEL.

ISBN-13: 978-1-4234-1356-1
ISBN-10: 1-4234-1356-3

HAL•LEONARD®
CORPORATION

7777 W. BLUEMOUND RD. P.O. BOX 13819 MILWAUKEE, WI 53213

In Australia Contact:
Hal Leonard Australia Pty. Ltd.
4 Lentara Court
Cheltenham, Victoria, 3192 Australia
Email: ausadmin@halleonard.com

Visit Hal Leonard Online at
www.halleonard.com

❶ CHRIST WAS BORN ON CHRISTMAS DAY

TENOR SAX

Traditional

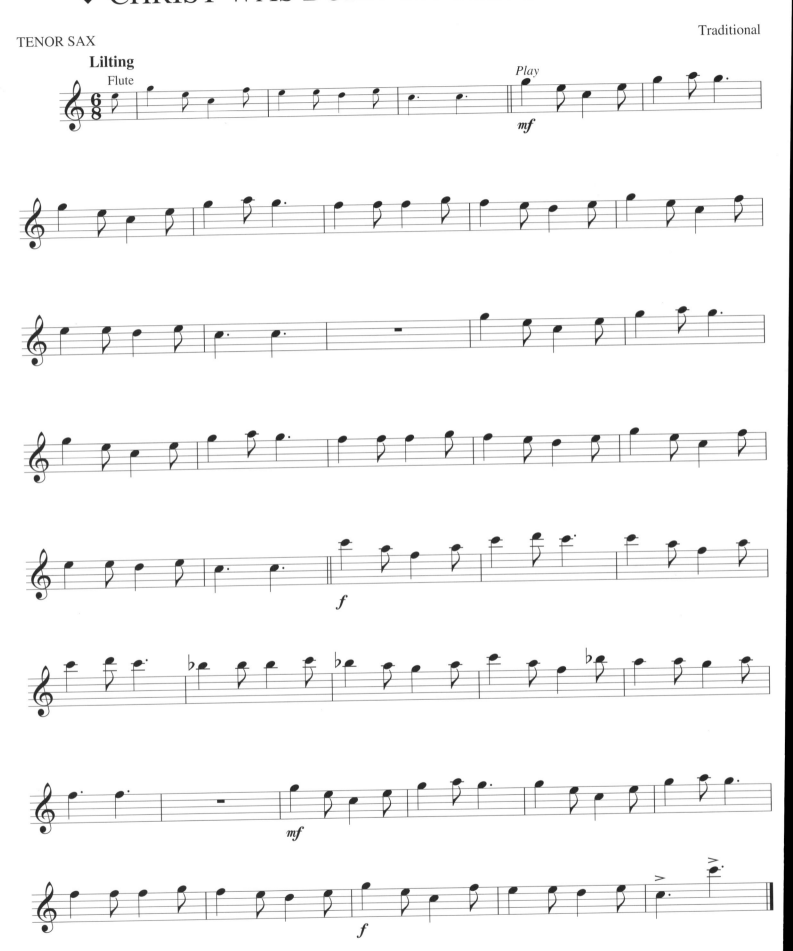

◆2 DECK THE HALL

TENOR SAX

Traditional Welsh Carol

4

◆③ THE FIRST NOEL

TENOR SAX

17th Century English Carol
Music from W. Sandys' *Christmas Carols*

small notes optional

f rit.

◆4 GOOD CHRISTIAN MEN, REJOICE

TENOR SAX

14th Century Latin Text
14th Century German Melody

◆ 5 GOOD KING WENCESLAS

Words by JOHN M. NEALE
Music from *Piae Cantiones*

TENOR SAX

With spirit

◆ HARK! THE HERALD ANGELS SING

TENOR SAX

Words by CHARLES WESLEY
Music by FELIX MENDELSSOHN-BARTHOLDY

❼ I HEARD THE BELLS ON CHRISTMAS DAY

TENOR SAX

Words by HENRY WADSWORTH LONGFELLOW
Music by JOHN BAPTISTE CALKIN

❽ IT CAME UPON THE MIDNIGHT CLEAR

TENOR SAX

Words by EDMUND HAMILTON SEARS
Music by RICHARD STORRS WILLIS

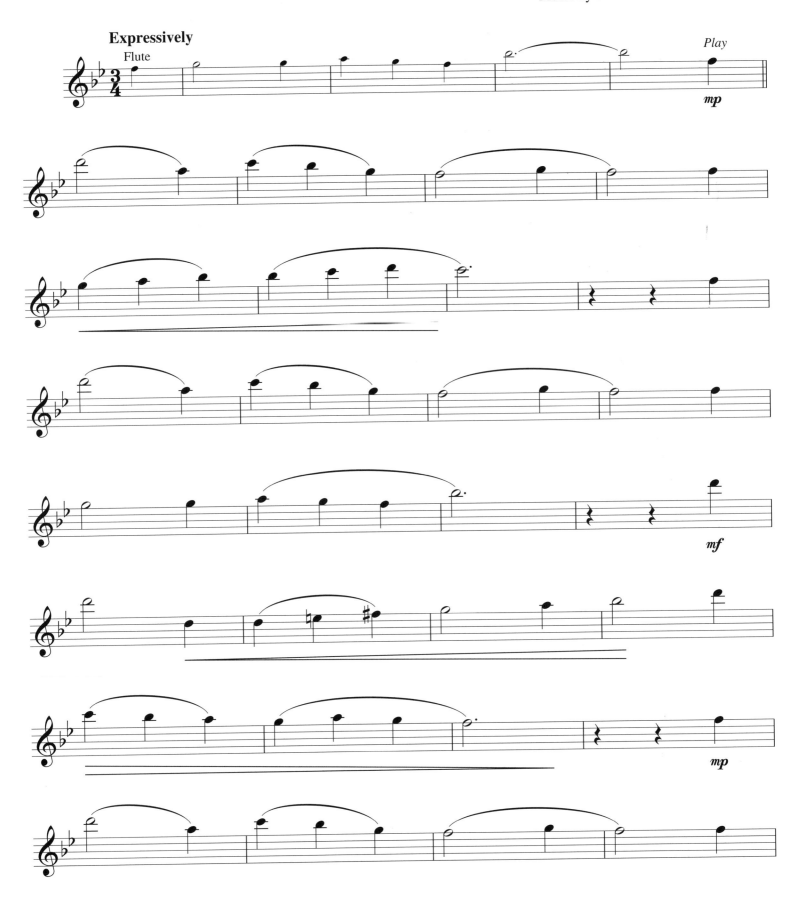

◆9 JOY TO THE WORLD

Words by ISAAC WATTS
Music by GEORGE FRIDERIC HANDEL

TENOR SAX

◆10 O CHRISTMAS TREE

TENOR SAX

Traditional German Carol

O COME, O COME, EMMANUEL

TENOR SAX

Plainsong, 13th Century

15

SING WE NOW OF CHRISTMAS

TENOR SAX

Traditional

Joyfully

◆14 WE THREE KINGS OF ORIENT ARE

TENOR SAX

Words and Music by
JOHN H. HOPKINS, JR.

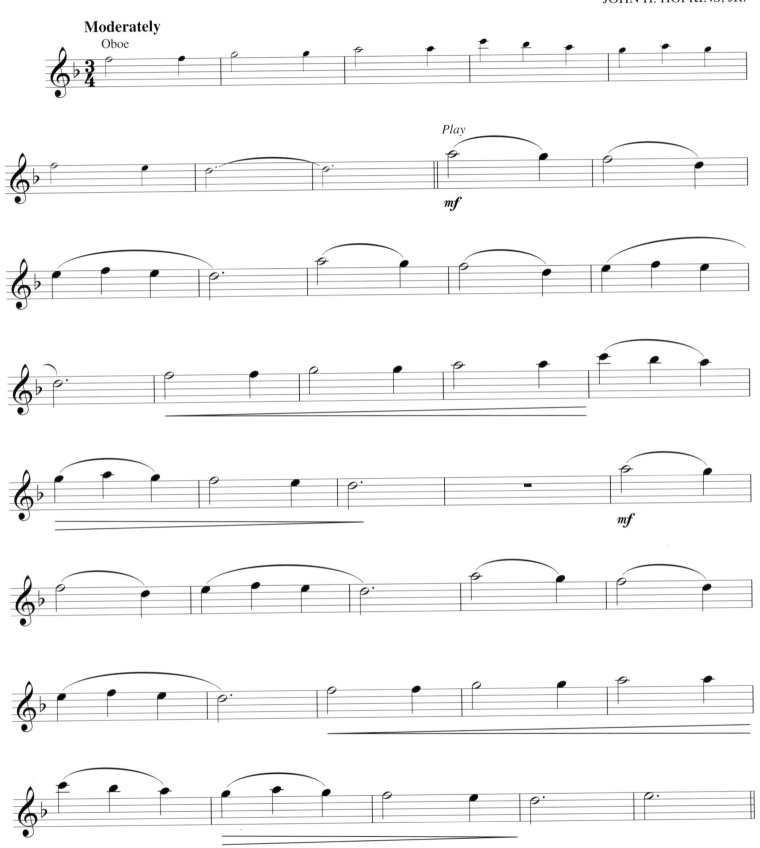

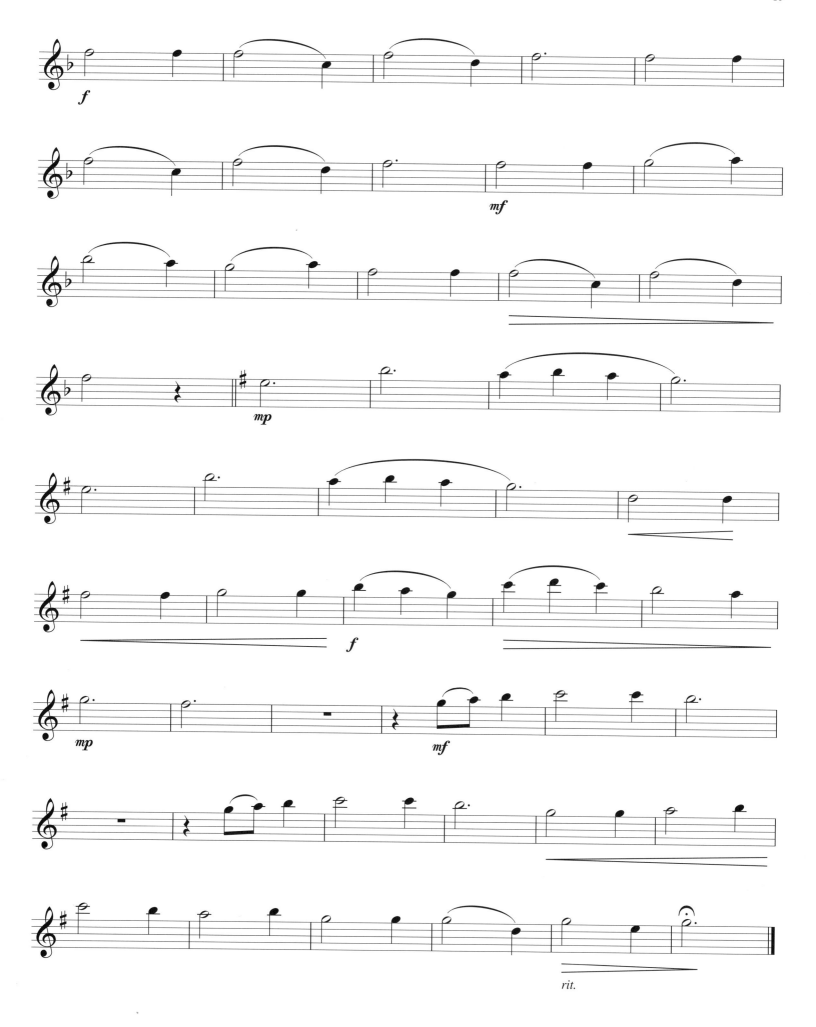

◆15 WE WISH YOU A MERRY CHRISTMAS

TENOR SAX

Traditional English Folksong

◆12 O LITTLE TOWN OF BETHLEHEM

TENOR SAX

Words by PHILLIPS BROOKS
Music by LEWIS H. REDNER

HAL•LEONARD INSTRUMENTAL PLAY-ALONG

WITH THESE FANTASTIC BOOK/CD PACKS, INSTRUMENTALISTS CAN PLAY ALONG WITH THEIR FAVORITE SONGS!

BROADWAY'S BEST

15 Broadway favorites arranged for the instrumentalist, including: Always Look on the Bright Side of Life • Any Dream Will Do • Castle on a Cloud • I Whistle a Happy Tune • My Favorite Things • Where Is Love? • and more.

00841974	Flute	$10.95
00841975	Clarinet	$10.95
00841976	Alto Sax	$10.95
00841977	Tenor Sax	$10.95
00841978	Trumpet	$10.95
00841979	Horn	$10.95
00841980	Trombone	$10.95
00841981	Violin	$10.95
00841982	Viola	$10.95
00841983	Cello	$10.95

CHRISTMAS CAROLS

15 favorites from the holidays, including: Deck the Hall • The First Noel • Good King Wenceslas • Hark! the Herald Angels Sing • It Came upon the Midnight Clear • O Christmas Tree • We Three Kings of Orient Are • and more.

00842132	Flute	$10.95
00842133	Clarinet	$10.95
00842134	Alto Sax	$10.95
00842135	Tenor Sax	$10.95
00842136	Trumpet	$10.95
00842137	Horn	$10.95
00842138	Trombone	$10.95
00842139	Violin	$10.95
00842140	Viola	$10.95
00842141	Cello	$10.95

CHRISTMAS FAVORITES

Includes 15 holiday favorites with a play-along CD: Blue Christmas • Caroling, Caroling • The Christmas Song (Chestnuts Roasting on an Open Fire) • Christmas Time Is Here • Do You Hear What I Hear • Here Comes Santa Claus (Right Down Santa Claus Lane) • (There's No Place Like) Home for the Holidays • I Saw Mommy Kissing Santa Claus • Little Saint Nick • Merry Christmas, Darling • O Bambino • Rudolph the Red-Nosed Reindeer • Santa Claus Is Comin' to Town • Snowfall

00841964	Flute	$10.95
00841965	Clarinet	$10.95
00841966	Alto Sax	$10.95
00841967	Tenor Sax	$10.95
00841968	Trumpet	$10.95
00841969	Horn	$10.95
00841970	Trombone	$10.95
00841971	Violin	$10.95
00841972	Viola	$10.95
00841973	Cello	$10.95

CLASSICAL FAVORITES

15 classic solos for all instrumentalists. Includes: Ave Maria (Schubert) • Blue Danube Waltz (Strauss, Jr.) • Für Elise (Beethoven) • Largo (Handel) • Minuet in G (Bach) • Ode to Joy (Beethoven) • Symphony No. 9 in E Minor ("From the New World"), Second Movement Excerpt (Dvorak) • and more.

00841954	Flute	$10.95
00841955	Clarinet	$10.95
00841956	Alto Sax	$10.95
00841957	Tenor Sax	$10.95
00841958	Trumpet	$10.95
00841959	Horn	$10.95
00841960	Trombone	$10.95
00841961	Violin	$10.95
00841962	Viola	$10.95
00841963	Cello	$10.95

CONTEMPORARY HITS

Play 15 of your pop favorites along with this great folio and full accompaniment CD. Songs include: Accidentally in Love • Calling All Angels • Don't Tell Me • Everything • Fallen • The First Cut Is the Deepest • Here Without You • Hey Ya! • If I Ain't Got You • It's My Life • 100 Years • Take My Breath Away (Love Theme) • This Love • White Flag • You Raise Me Up.

00841924	Flute	$12.95
00841925	Clarinet	$12.95
00841926	Alto Sax	$12.95
00841927	Tenor Sax	$10.95
00841928	Trumpet	$10.95
00841929	Horn	$10.95
00841930	Trombone	$10.95
00841931	Violin	$12.95
00841932	Viola	$12.95
00841933	Cello	$10.95

DISNEY GREATS

Another great play-along collection of 15 Disney favorites, including: Arabian Nights • A Change in Me • Hawaiian Roller Coaster Ride • I'm Still Here (Jim's Theme) • It's a Small World • Look Through My Eyes • Supercalifragilisticexpialidocious • Where the Dream Takes You • Yo Ho (A Pirate's Life for Me) • and more.

00841934	Flute	$12.95
00842078	Oboe	$12.95
00841935	Clarinet	$12.95
00841936	Alto Sax	$12.95
00841937	Tenor Sax	$12.95
00841938	Trumpet	$12.95
00841939	Horn	$12.95
00841940	Trombone	$12.95
00841941	Violin	$12.95
00841942	Viola	$12.95
00841943	Cello	$12.95

ESSENTIAL ROCK

Instrumentalists will love jamming with a play-along CD for 15 top rock classics, including: Aqualung • Brown Eyed Girl • Crocodile Rock • Don't Stop • Free Bird • I Want to Want Me • La Grange • Low Rider • Maggie May • Walk This Way • and more.

00841944	Flute	$10.95
00841945	Clarinet	$10.95
00841946	Alto Sax	$10.95
00841947	Tenor Sax	$10.95
00841948	Trumpet	$10.95
00841949	Horn	$10.95
00841950	Trombone	$10.95
00841951	Violin	$10.95
00841952	Viola	$10.95
00841953	Cello	$10.95

HIGH SCHOOL MUSICAL

Solo arrangements with CD accompaniment for 9 hits from the wildly popular Disney Channel original movie. Songs include: Bop to the Top • Breaking Free • Get'cha Head in the Game • I Can't Take My Eyes Off of You • Start of Something New • Stick to the Status Quo • We're All in This Together • What I've Been Looking For • When There Was Me and You.

00842121	Flute	$10.95
00842122	Clarinet	$10.95
00842123	Alto Sax	$10.95
00842124	Tenor Sax	$10.95
00842125	Trumpet	$10.95
00842126	Horn	$10.95
00842127	Trombone	$10.95
00842128	Violin	$10.95
00842129	Viola	$10.95
00842130	Cello	$10.95

ANDREW LLOYD WEBBER CLASSICS

12 solos from Webber's greatest shows complete with full band accompaniment on CD. Titles include: As If We Never Said Goodbye • Close Every Door • Don't Cry for Me Argentina • Everything's Alright • Go Go Go Joseph • Gus: The Theatre Cat • Love Changes Everything • The Music of the Night • Our Kind of Love • The Phantom of the Opera • Unexpected Song • Whistle Down the Wind.

00841824	Flute	$14.95
00841825	Oboe	$14.95
00841826	Clarinet	$14.95
00841827	Alto Sax	$14.95
00841828	Tenor Sax	$14.95
00841829	Trumpet	$14.95
00841830	Horn	$14.95
00841831	Trombone	$14.95
00841832	Mallet Percussion	$14.95
00841833	Violin	$14.95
00841834	Viola	$14.95
00841835	Cello	$14.95

MOVIE MUSIC

15 hits from popular movie blockbusters of today, including: And All That Jazz • Come What May • I Am a Man of Constant Sorrow • I Believe I Can Fly • I Walk the Line • Seasons of Love • Theme from Spider Man • and more

00842089	Flute	$10.95
00842090	Clarinet	$10.95
00842091	Alto Sax	$10.95
00842092	Tenor Sax	$10.95
00842093	Trumpet	$10.95
00842094	Horn	$10.95
00842095	Trombone	$10.95
00842096	Violin	$10.95
00842097	Viola	$10.95
00842098	Cello	$10.95

TV FAVORITES

15 TV tunes arranged for instrumentalists, including: The Addams Family Theme • The Brady Bunch • Green Acres Theme • Happy Days • Johnny's Theme • Linus and Lucy • NFL on Fox Theme • Theme from The Simpsons • and more.

00842079	Flute	$10.95
00842080	Clarinet	$10.95
00842081	Alto Sax	$10.95
00842082	Tenor Sax	$10.95
00842083	Trumpet	$10.95
00842084	Horn	$10.95
00842085	Trombone	$10.95
00842086	Violin	$10.95
00842087	Viola	$10.95
00842088	Cello	$10.95

FOR MORE INFORMATION, SEE YOUR LOCAL MUSIC DEALER, OR WRITE TO:

HAL•LEONARD® CORPORATION

7777 W. BLUEMOUND RD. P.O. BOX 13819 MILWAUKEE, WI 53213

PRICES, CONTENTS AND AVAILABILITY ARE SUBJECT TO CHANGE WITHOUT NOTICE.

SOME PRODUCTS MAY NOT BE AVAILABLE OUTSIDE THE U.S.A.

DISNEY CHARACTERS AND ARTWORK © DISNEY ENTERPRISES, INC.

VISIT HAL LEONARD ONLINE AT
WWW.HALLEONARD.COM